SACRED DAYS, SACRED SONGS

A Holy Week Devotional

Sacred Days, Sacred Songs

A Holy Week Devotional

Michael D. Young

SHADOW
MOUNTAIN
PUBLISHING

Visit us at shadowmountain.com

Library of Congress Cataloging-in-Publication Data

Names: Young, Michael, 1984– author.
Title: Sacred days, sacred songs: a Holy Week devotional / Michael D. Young.
Description: [Salt Lake City]: Shadow Mountain, [2024]. | Performances by The Tabernacle Choir at Temple Square and Gentri. | Includes bibliographical references. | Summary: "Author Michael D. Young relates the stories behind sixteen beloved songs about Jesus Christ in a format that lends itself to reading about two songs per day for Holy Week. Contains QR codes linking to performances of the songs, most by The Tabernacle Choir at Temple Square"—Provided by publisher.
Identifiers: LCCN 2023036174 (print) | LCCN 2023036175 (ebook) | ISBN 9781639932290 (hardback) | ISBN 9781649332462 (ebook)
Subjects: LCSH: Holy Week music—History and criticism. | Holy Week—Prayers and devotions. | BISAC: RELIGION / Holidays / Easter & Lent
Classification: LCC ML3186. Y68 2024 (print) | LCC ML3186 (ebook) | DDC 264/.23—dc23/eng/20230802
LC record available at https://lccn.loc.gov/2023036174
LC ebook record available at https://lccn.loc.gov/2023036175

Printed in China
RR Donnelley, Dongguan, China

10 9 8 7 6 5 4 3 2 1

"I am the resurrection, and the life:
he that believeth in me, though he
were dead, yet shall he live."

—JOHN 11:25

CONTENTS

ACKNOWLEDGMENTS

I know and love many of the songs I feature in this book thanks to the efforts my mother made to keep me involved in music from a young age. From piano lessons to church choirs—which she often directed—wonderful music constantly surrounded me.

I'd be remiss if I didn't mention the many choir directors I had in high school and beyond. Ms. Elizabeth Bassler, Mr. David Barthelmess, and Dr. Rosalind Hall were particularly impactful in musical development. I also thank Dr. Mack Wilberg and Dr. Ryan Murphy for broadening my Easter repertoire and giving me so many opportunities to take part in glorious performances of it with The Tabernacle Choir at Temple Square.

It is my hope that this book will help others gain a deeper appreciation for celebrating Easter through music.

INTRODUCTION

Biblical prophets spoke for generations about God's promise to gather and deliver His people through the sacrifice of a Savior. Indeed, many years before Jesus's birth, the prophet Isaiah wrote of the coming Messiah, "For unto us a child is born, unto us a son is given: and the government shall be upon his shoulder: and his name shall be called Wonderful, Counsellor, The mighty God, The everlasting Father, The Prince of Peace" (Isaiah 9:6).

While Christmas celebrates the birth of Jesus, Easter is the time to celebrate the fulfillment of His life and mission.

At the beginning of Jesus's mortal ministry, He specifically pointed to how His life and work would fulfill those ancient prophecies, including this one from Isaiah:

"The Spirit of the Lord God is upon me; because the Lord hath anointed me to preach good tidings unto the meek; he hath sent me to bind up the brokenhearted, to proclaim liberty to the captives, and the opening of the prison to them that are bound; to proclaim the acceptable year of the Lord, and the day of vengeance of our God; to comfort all that mourn; . . . to give unto them beauty for ashes" (Isaiah 61:1–3; see also Luke 4:16–21).

When Jesus declared Himself the fulfillment of that prophecy, He was telling the world that the babe in the manger had grown into a man who would heal the sick, raise the dead, preach the gospel, and most importantly, give Himself as a sacrifice for the sins of all humankind.

What, then, is an appropriate way to celebrate such a sacrifice and such a season? For centuries, the answer for Christian congregations has been to raise their voices in song. As the author Victor Hugo once said of music, "Music expresses that which cannot be said and on which it is impossible to be silent." I find that is particularly true during Easter. Words alone simply do not do justice in expressing the deep emotions the faithful feel when thinking about our Savior. But when those words are set to music, the resulting hymns can invite us to ponder the deep meaning and importance of this joyful season.

While many Christmas songs feature words of joyful anticipation, looking forward to the realization of future blessings, many Easter songs focus on celebrating Christ's immense and eternal victory over sin and death. The Easter season gives us an opportunity to ponder the events of the Holy Week and consider what they might mean to us individually and to the world as a whole.

Each section of this book highlights a different day of the Holy Week, which begins on Palm Sunday and ends on Easter Sunday. For each day, I have highlighted an attribute of the Savior's character—including deliverance, compassion, grace, hope, love, sacrifice, obedience, and renewal—along with some scriptures to ponder.

Along with the scriptures are two sacred songs that accompany the theme. The songs are selected from many that are traditionally sung during Holy Week celebrations throughout the Christian world. My hope is that as you focus on these beautiful expressions of faith, you can deepen your appreciation and love for the Savior and feel motivated to develop these traits in your own life.

For each song, I present the lyrics and share a little of the history and origin of the song. At the end of each song, a QR code will link to a YouTube performance of that song for you and your family to enjoy—and maybe even to sing along with!

Easter is a time to celebrate the greatest news of the gospel: "He is not here: for he is risen" (Matthew 28:6).

DAY ONE

PALM SUNDAY

DELIVERANCE

"Rejoice greatly, O daughter of Zion;
shout, O daughter of Jerusalem: behold,
thy King cometh unto thee: he is just, and
having salvation; lowly, and riding upon an
ass, and upon a colt the foal of an ass."

ZECHARIAH 9:9

"And many spread their garments in the way:
and others cut down branches off the trees,
and strawed them in the way. And they that
went before, and they that followed, cried,
saying, Hosanna; Blessed is he that cometh in
the name of the Lord: Blessed be the kingdom
of our father David, that cometh in the name
of the Lord: Hosanna in the highest."

MARK 11:8–10

The Deliverer

Throughout Jesus's ministry, He offered deliverance to many who suffered from physical and mental afflictions, including restoring sight to the blind and casting out evil spirits. He delivered individuals from their sins by forgiving them. He even delivered Lazarus from death itself. But these instances were only a prelude to the ultimate deliverance Jesus would bring in His role as the Messiah.

While many people during the Savior's lifetime were looking for a deliverer who would save them from Roman oppression, Jesus Christ offered something much more profound. When Jesus entered Jerusalem on Palm Sunday, the people cried "Hosanna!"—which means "Save us now!"—pleading with Him for deliverance. Within that week, He did. His passage through the Atonement, the Crucifixion, and the Resurrection were the keys required to deliver all mankind from both sin and death—a deliverance that can bless us even today.

THE HOLY CITY

Lyrics

Last night I lay a-sleeping
There came a dream so fair;
I stood in old Jerusalem
Beside the temple there.

I heard the children singing,
And ever as they sang
Methought the voice of angels
From Heaven in answer rang:

"Jerusalem! Jerusalem!
"Lift up your gates and sing!
"Hosanna in the highest!
"Hosanna to your King!"

And then methought my dream was chang'd.
The streets no longer rang.
Hush'd were the glad Hosannas
The little children sang.

The sun grew dark with mystery.
The morn was cold and chill.
As the shadow of a cross arose
Upon a lonely hill.

"Jerusalem! Jerusalem!
"Hark! How the angels sing!
"Hosanna in the highest!
"Hosanna to your King!"

And once again the scene was chang'd.
New earth there seem'd to be.
I saw the Holy City
Beside the tideless sea.

The light of God was on its streets.
The gates were open wide,
And all who would might enter
And no one was denied.

No need of moon or stars by night
Or sun to shine by day.
It was the new Jerusalem
That would not pass away.

"Jerusalem! Jerusalem!
"Sing for the night is o'er!
"Hosanna in the highest!
"Hosanna for evermore!"

https://authormichaelyoung.com
/sacred-days-sacred-songs/

History

Frederic Weatherly was an Oxford-educated lawyer in England who wrote more than 3,000 songs during his lifetime, many of which became famous and are still beloved today, including "The Holy City" and the perennially popular "Danny Boy."

Weatherly often drew inspiration for his lyrics from biblical passages, and, in the case of "The Holy City," he turned to the book of Revelation after being inspired by a sermon offered by Reverend Stephen G. Haskins. Moved by Haskins's words, Weatherly was inspired to write a hymn that celebrated the New Jerusalem, with its streets of gold, gates of pearl, and river of life. The holy city is a place of beauty and majesty, where the faithful will reunite with their loved ones who have passed away.

The title of the song appears in Revelation 21:2, "And I John saw the holy city, new Jerusalem, coming down from God out of heaven, prepared as a bride adorned for her husband." Another verse of the hymn clearly draws inspiration from Revelation 22:5, "And there shall be no night there; and they need no candle, neither light of the sun; for the Lord God giveth them light: and they shall reign for ever and ever."

Weatherly wrote the lyrics in just a few days and then

collaborated with his friend Michael Maybrick to compose the music. The song appeared in 1892 and quickly gained popularity in both England and the United States. It was so beloved that it was often sung at the memorials for fallen soldiers during World War I. Today, it remains a common choice for funerals and other religious meetings.

ALL GLORY, LAUD, AND HONOR

Lyrics

All glory, laud, and honor
To you, Redeemer, King,
To whom the lips of children
Made sweet hosannas ring.

You are the King of Israel
And David's royal Son,
Now in the Lord's name coming,
The King and Blessed One.

The company of angels
Is praising you on high;

And we with all creation
In chorus make reply.

The people of the Hebrews
With palms before you went;
Our praise and prayer and anthems
Before you we present.

To you before your passion,
They sang their hymns of praise;
To you, now high exalted,
Our melody we raise.

As you received their praises,
Accept the prayers we bring,
For you delight in goodness,
O good and gracious King!

https://authormichaelyoung.com
/sacred-days-sacred-songs/

History

This hymn began as a Latin text, "Gloria, laus, et honor," written in the ninth century by St. Theodulf of Orleans, who wrote it as a processional chant for Palm Sunday. It is sometimes called "Hosanna, Loud

Hosanna." The lyrics and its joyful melody bring to mind what the crowd cried out during Jesus's triumphal entry into Jerusalem on that special Sunday.

The Latin version of the song passed down through Christian believers until 1854 when John Mason Neale, a hymnologist and Anglican priest, translated it into English and paired it with the tune we sing today.

Neale wrote many other hymns, including the popular "Good Christian Men, Rejoice," as well as being a prolific translator of ancient and medieval hymns. His ability to remain faithful to the original texts and set them to familiar tunes helped popularize many hymns that might have otherwise been lost or forgotten.

Throughout his career as an Anglican priest, Neale was deeply committed to the revival of ancient Christian practices and the restoration of the Catholic tradition within the Anglican church. He founded the Society of Saint Margaret, a religious community of women dedicated to serving the poor and sick, and he also established a publishing house, the Ecclesiological Society, which promoted the study of church architecture and art.

"All Glory, Laud, and Honor" allows each of us to picture ourselves in the crowd welcoming Jesus into Jerusalem with joyful shouts of "Hosanna!"

DAY TWO

HOLY MONDAY

COMPASSION

"And Jesus went about all the cities and villages, teaching in their synagogues, and preaching the gospel of the kingdom, and healing every sickness and every disease among the people. But when he saw the multitudes, he was moved with compassion on them, because they fainted, and were scattered abroad, as sheep having no shepherd."

MATTHEW 9:35–36

"Now when he came nigh to the gate of the city, behold, there was a dead man carried out, the only son of his mother, and she was a widow: and much people of the city was with her. And when the Lord saw her, he had compassion on her, and said unto her, Weep not. And he came and touched the bier: and they that bare him stood still. And he said, Young man, I say unto thee, Arise. And he that was dead sat up, and began to speak. And he delivered him to his mother."

LUKE 7:12–15

Suffering With

The Savior's compassion was boundless, especially toward those who approached Him with a repentant heart. He not only healed their physical problems, but their souls as well.

The Latin root of the word *compassion* means "to suffer with." Throughout His life, the Savior showed compassion for people from all walks of life as He tended to those who were sick, or who had been excluded from society. He cleansed lepers, restoring their health and allowing them to rejoin society.

When Lazarus died, Jesus suffered with the family, weeping with those in mourning, even though He knew He had power to raise Lazarus from the dead.

He felt compassion for the sinner who wanted to mend her ways.

He showed compassion for a woman who had lived a sinful life, but who came to Him and washed His feet with her tears.

More than once, he showed compassion toward those whose physical needs were not being met, including multiplying a few loaves and fishes to feed thousands of hungry people.

We can be blessed today by the Savior's compassion by "suffering with" those who need our help.

DROP, DROP, SLOW TEARS

Lyrics

Drop, drop, slow tears,
And bathe those beauteous feet,
Which brought from heav'n
The news and Prince of Peace.

Cease not, wet eyes,
His mercies to entreat;
To cry for vengeance
Sin doth never cease.

In your deep floods,
Drown all my faults and fears;
Nor let His eye
See sin, but through my tears.

https://authormichaelyoung.com
/sacred-days-sacred-songs/

History

This hymn paints a picture of a repentant sinner coming to the Savior and bathing His feet in his tears, much like the woman did in Luke 7:37–50. The song pledges that we will quickly repent of our sins—"through my tears"—and return to Christ a humble heart.

"Drop, Drop, Slow Tears" was written in the early seventeenth century by Phineas Fletcher, an English poet and cleric, and became one of his most famous works. The hymn's haunting, mournful melody, thought to have been written by Orlando Gibbons, adds a solemnity to this enduring piece of sacred music, which is often sung during Holy Week as it beautifully expresses the longing the faithful feel for the redeeming power of Christ.

Phineas Fletcher was born in 1582, the son of a Puritan minister. After completing his religious studies, Fletcher became a minister himself and served in several parishes in England.

Fletcher's poetry was influenced by the metaphysical poets of his time, like John Donne, and he was known for his use of complex metaphors and intricate language. "Drop, Drop, Slow Tears" was first published in his collection of poems, *Sospetto d'Herode*, in 1620. His poetry was also admired by writers John Milton and Samuel

Johnson, and his influence can be seen in the work of later poets John Keats and T. S. Eliot.

O DIVINE REDEEMER

Lyrics

Ah! turn me not away,
Receive me, tho' unworthy;
Hear Thou my cry, hear Thou my cry,
Behold, Lord, my distress.

Answer me from Thy throne.
Haste Thee, Lord, to mine aid.
Thy pity shew in my deep anguish.

Let not the sword of vengeance smite me,
Though righteous Thine anger, O Lord.
Shield me in danger! O regard me,
On Thee, Lord alone, will I call.

O Divine Redeemer!
I pray Thee, grant me pardon,
And remember not my sins.
Forgive me, O Divine Redeemer!

Night gathers round my soul.
Fearful, I cry to Thee!
Come to my aid, O Lord!
Haste Thee, Lord, haste to help me.
Hear my cry, save me, Lord in Thy mercy
Come and save me, O Lord!

O Divine Redeemer!
I pray Thee, grant me pardon,
And remember not, remember not,
O Lord, my sins.

Save in the day of retribution;
From Death shield Thou me, O my God!
O Divine Redeemer! Have mercy!
Help me, my Savior.

https://authormichaelyoung.com
/sacred-days-sacred-songs/

History

"O Divine Redeemer" was written by Charles Gounod, and its prayerful plea for redemption and forgiveness makes it a popular choice to sing during Easter. The dramatic accompaniment and the song's rising intensity create a distinctly operatic feel that takes the listener through a musical journey. Though Gounod originally wrote the song as a solo for a mezzo-soprano, it has since been turned into a choral piece.

Gounod is perhaps most famous for his operas of *Faust* and *Romeo and Juliet*, and his setting of "Ave Maria." He viewed his work as expressions and extensions of his faith. One historian said of him, "He could as readily write a sermon as an opera." "O Divine Redeemer" is a bit of both.

After a successful career, Gounod entered semiretirement. During this time, his five-year-old grandson passed away suddenly, and in his intense grief, Gounod turned once again to writing sacred music, including a requiem for his departed grandson.

"O Divine Redeemer" was also written during this time of deep spiritual reflection. Some people have suggested that Gounod wrote the hymn after attending a play about the life of Mary Magdalene and being inspired by a scene in which she sings a prayer for forgiveness.

Originally written in French, the song was known as "Repentir: Scene sous forme de priere," which translates to "Repentance: Scene in the form of a prayer." Gounod was in poor health while writing the music, completing it only six months before his death of a stroke. Many people consider this hymn his ultimate expression of faith. His grandson's requiem remained unfinished.

DAY THREE

HOLY TUESDAY

GRACE

"Let us therefore come boldly unto the throne of grace, that we may obtain mercy, and find grace to help in time of need."

HEBREWS 4:16

"We believe that through the grace of the Lord Jesus Christ we shall be saved."

ACTS 15:11

The Power of Grace

Jesus's grace is a power that grants us divine help or strength in our times of need. Its power stems from the mercy and love of Jesus, and it—coupled with the blessings of Jesus's Atonement—can save us when we have nowhere else to turn. Grace is a gift that extends beyond what we can do for ourselves.

The Gospel of John recounts the story of a woman taken in adultery. Under the law, she should have been stoned to death, yet the Savior offers an unexpected reply to her would-be executioners: "He that is without sin among you, let him first cast a stone at her" (John 8:7). When this woman had nowhere else to turn, the Son of God did not condemn her, but gave her a gracious opportunity to reform her life. On a day when she could have lost her life, she instead found a new life through the grace of Jesus.

The Savior's ever-present power of grace is still available to us all as we reach out our hands to Him.

AMAZING GRACE

Lyrics

Amazing grace, how sweet the sound
That saved a wretch like me!
I once was lost, but now I am found
Was blind, but now I see.

'Twas grace that taught my heart to fear
And grace my fears relieved.
How precious did that grace appear
The hour I first believed!

Through many dangers, toils and snares,
We have already come.
'Tis grace has brought us safe thus far
And grace will lead us home.

When we've been there ten thousand years
Bright shining as the sun.
We've no less days to sing God's praise
Than when we've first begun.

Amazing grace, how sweet the sound
That saved a wretch like me!
I once was lost, but now I am found
Was blind, but now I see.

https://authormichaelyoung.com
/sacred-days-sacred-songs/

History

"Amazing Grace" was written in 1772 by John Newton, a man who underwent an incredible spiritual journey from sinner to respected priest.

John was only seven years old when his staunchly religious Puritan mother died. When he was eleven, his father, a sea captain, took him aboard his ship, which resulted in John spending most of his formative years with unruly, drunken sailors. He later described his younger self with these words, "How industrious is Satan served. I was formerly one of his active undertemptors and had my influence been equal to my wishes, I would have carried all the human race with me. A common drunkard or profligate is a petty sinner to what I was."

He was later conscripted into the British navy, and when he tried to desert, he was caught and whipped eight dozen times. While he was serving on another ship, he got along so poorly with the crew that they left him on the coast of West Africa, where he was enslaved. He was later rescued at the request of his father.

While on his way home, however, his ship was caught in a terrible storm, and John, fearing for his life, prayed to God to save them. After his prayer, some of the ship's cargo shifted in exactly the right way to plug a hole in the hull, allowing them to safely reach the shore. This experience started him on his journey toward Christianity, though his conversion didn't happen all at once.

"I cannot consider myself to have been a believer in the full sense of the word, until a considerable time afterward," he later wrote.

He continued as a sailor for some time until suffering a stroke in 1754. Ten years later, he became an Anglican priest and began writing his own hymns to accompany his services. He wrote 280 hymns, including "Amazing Grace," which he penned for the New Year's Day service of 1773. It is unclear if the accompanying music was written at the same time or if the lyrics were simply chanted.

The song was first printed in *Olney Hymns* in 1779, and though it didn't find an audience in England for some time, its popularity grew dramatically in the United States. It was a favorite of Methodist and Baptist preachers during the nineteenth century's Second Great Awakening in the United States. While the tune we sing today—called NEW BRITAIN—was first used by William

Walker in 1835, the lyrics have been set to more than twenty different tunes over the years.

In 1788, John published a now well-known pamphlet that shed light on the horrible conditions aboard the ships that were used to enslave those who were violently stolen from Africa: "It will always be a subject of humiliating reflection to me, that I was once an active instrument in a business at which my heart now shudders." The English government outlawed slavery in Great Britain in 1807, the year of John's death.

Today, "Amazing Grace" has become emblematic of African American faith and was also popularized during the civil rights movement because of its liberatory symbolism. It is one of the most popular hymns in the English-speaking world. It has been featured on more than 11,000 albums, including some from legendary artists Aretha Franklin, Elvis Presley, Ray Charles, Mahalia Jackson, and Johnny Cash.

Come, Thou Fount
of Every Blessing

Lyrics

Come, Thou Fount of every blessing,
Tune my heart to sing Thy grace.
Streams of mercy, never ceasing,
Call for songs of loudest praise.

Teach me some melodious sonnet,
Sung by flaming tongues above;
Praise the mount, I'm fixed upon it,
Mount of Thy redeeming love.

Here I raise my Ebenezer,
Hither by Thy help I'm come;
And I hope, by Thy good pleasure,
Safely to arrive at home.

Jesus sought me when a stranger,
Wand'ring from the fold of God.
He, to rescue me from danger
Interposed His precious blood.

O to grace, how great a debtor,
Daily I'm constrained to be!

Let Thy goodness, like a fetter,
Bind my wand'ring heart to Thee.

Prone to wander, Lord, I feel it,
Prone to leave the God I love.
Here's my heart, O take and seal it,
Seal it for Thy courts above.

O that day when freed from sinning,
I shall see Thy lovely face.
Clothed then in the blood-washed linen,
How I'll sing Thy sovereign grace.

Come, my Lord, no longer tarry.
Take my ransomed soul away!
Send Thine angels now to carry
Me to realms of endless day.

https://authormichaelyoung.com
/sacred-days-sacred-songs/

History

    This hymn compares the Savior to a fountain from which all blessings flow. Just as normal water is essential to sustain life, the "living water" Jesus offers us is essential to our spiritual life.

Robert Robinson was born in England in 1735, the son of a poor farmer. He grew up with little education, and his difficult childhood led him down a path of sin and debauchery. When he was twenty, however, he found religion, atoned for his wayward youth, and eventually became a Baptist minister.

In 1757, Robinson wrote the words to "Come, Thou Fount of Every Blessing." The melody is believed to have been composed by John Wyeth, a fellow Christian and music publisher who included the hymn in his 1813 hymnal, *Repository of Sacred Music, Part Second.*

The hymn quickly became popular, and it has since been translated into many languages. It is still sung by Christians around the world today.

Despite his success as a minister and hymnist, Robinson struggled with his faith, and eventually became disillusioned with organized religion. It is said that when he heard this hymn later in his life, he said, "I wrote that hymn many years ago, and I would give anything to experience again the feeling I had when I wrote it."

Robinson's life is a reminder that we are all "prone to wander" and that we all must rely on the Savior's daily grace to keep our faith alive.

HOLY WEDNESDAY

HOPE

"But they that wait upon the Lord shall renew
their strength; they shall mount up with
wings as eagles; they shall run, and not be
weary; and they shall walk, and not faint."

ISAIAH 40:31

"Jesus said unto her, I am the resurrection,
and the life: he that believeth in me, though
he were dead, yet shall he live: and whosoever
liveth and believeth in me shall never die."

JOHN 11:25–26

Bestowing Hope

One of Jesus's greatest gifts is hope.

When His disciples were trapped in a powerful storm that threatened to sink their vessel, Jesus offered them hope. With a few words, Jesus stilled the boisterous waves, turning a dangerous situation into one of complete safety. When Jesus is near, we do not need to fear the future.

When Jesus knew that His time in mortality was coming to a close, He comforted His disciples by telling them, "I will pray the Father, and he shall give you another Comforter, that he may abide with you for ever. . . . I will not leave you comfortless: I will come to you" (John 14:16, 18). He knew the fierce persecution the disciples would soon face but reassured them with hope for the future.

His message of hope endures today with the promise that "God shall wipe away all tears from their eyes; and there shall be no more death, neither sorrow, nor crying, neither shall there be any more pain: for the former things are passed away" (Revelation 21:4).

IT IS WELL WITH MY SOUL

Lyrics

When peace, like a river, attendeth my way,
When sorrows like sea billows roll;
Whatever my lot, Thou hast taught me to say,
It is well, it is well, with my soul.

It is well (it is well), with my soul (with my soul),
It is well, it is well, with my soul!

Though Satan should buffet, though trials should come,
Let this blest assurance control,
That Christ has regarded my helpless estate,
And hath shed His own blood for my soul.

It is well (it is well), with my soul (with my soul),
It is well, it is well, with my soul!

My sin, oh, the bliss of this glorious thought!
My sin, not in part but the whole,
Is nailed to the cross, and I bear it no more,
Praise the Lord, praise the Lord, O my soul.

It is well (it is well), with my soul (with my soul),
It is well, it is well, with my soul!

And Lord, haste the day when my faith shall be sight,
The clouds be rolled back as a scroll;
The trump shall resound, and the Lord shall descend,
Even so, it is well with my soul.

It is well (it is well), with my soul (with my soul),
It is well, it is well, with my soul!

https://authormichaelyoung.com
/sacred-days-sacred-songs/

History

This stirring hymn has a tragic history. Horatio Spafford was a business owner who had fallen on hard times following the Great Chicago Fire of 1871. After a difficult year, he wanted to spend a beautiful Christmas season with his wife and three daughters in Paris. He sent his wife and daughters across the sea on an ocean liner while he stayed behind to finish up some business.

Partway through the voyage, however, the ship his family was on collided with another ship in the middle of the ocean and sank. Horatio's wife was able to cling to some floating debris long enough to be rescued from the bone-chilling water. When she arrived in Paris, she sent a message back to her husband: "Saved alone." All three of their daughters had drowned.

A short time later, Horatio made the same trip across the ocean. While standing on the deck one night, the captain informed Horatio that they were passing the spot where the other ship had gone down with his family. Moved by the scene, Horatio was inspired to write a poem that began with the words "When peace, like a river, attendeth my way, when sorrows like sea billows roll"—a poem of hope and of trust that he would see his loved ones again.

He reunited with his wife, and the two of them lived lives of philanthropy and charity, including founding a center to take care of orphans. Despite the Spaffords' tragedy, they rose above their sadness and brought hope and comfort to others in need.

"It Is Well with My Soul" was eventually set to music and was published in 1876 by Ira Sankey and Philip Bliss. It has been included in many hymnbooks and provides comfort to countless people who also find "sorrows like sea billows [rolling]" in their lives.

THE SOLID ROCK
(MY HOPE IS BUILT ON NOTHING LESS)

Lyrics

My hope is built on nothing less
Than Jesus' blood and righteousness;
I dare not trust the sweetest frame,
But wholly lean on Jesus' name.

On Christ, the solid Rock, I stand:
All other ground is sinking sand;
All other ground is sinking sand.

When darkness veils His lovely face,
I rest on His unchanging grace;
In every high and stormy gale,
My anchor holds within the veil.

On Christ, the solid Rock, I stand:
All other ground is sinking sand;
All other ground is sinking sand.

His oath, His covenant, His blood,
Support me in the whelming flood;

When all around my soul gives way,
He then is all my hope and stay.

On Christ, the solid Rock, I stand:
All other ground is sinking sand;
All other ground is sinking sand.

When He shall come with trumpet sound,
O may I then in Him be found:
Dressed in His righteousness alone,
Faultless to stand before the throne.

On Christ, the solid Rock, I stand:
All other ground is sinking sand;
All other ground is sinking sand.

https://authormichaelyoung.com
/sacred-days-sacred-songs/

History

"The Solid Rock" is a popular Christian hymn that is also frequently known by its opening line: "My hope is built on nothing less." The hymn was written in 1834 by Edward Mote, a British pastor and hymn writer.

Mote was born in London, England, in 1797 and worked as a cabinetmaker and carpenter. He converted to Christianity at eighteen and began preaching in his mid-twenties.

While serving as the pastor at Rehoboth Baptist Chapel in Horsham, England, Mote penned the lyrics to "The Solid Rock" under its original title, "The Immutable Basis of a Sinner's Hope." It was published in a collection of hymns that Mote compiled with a fellow pastor.

The lyrics of "The Solid Rock" are based on Matthew 7:24–27, in which Jesus tells a parable known as "the wise man and the foolish man." The verses describe two builders, one who built his house on a rock and another who built his house on sand. Mote's hymn emphasizes the importance of building one's life on the "solid rock" of Jesus Christ, instead of the "shifting sand" of worldly philosophies. Those who build on Christ's rock may find lasting hope, while those who do not will find no substitution.

The hymn quickly became popular in England, and it was eventually introduced to the United States in the mid-nineteenth century. The tune that is most associated with the hymn was written by William Bradbury, an American composer, in 1863.

Today, "The Solid Rock" is still sung in Christian churches around the world and is a reminder that genuine hope comes only through Christ.

DAY FIVE

MAUNDY THURSDAY

LOVE

"This is my commandment, That ye love
one another, as I have loved you. Greater
love hath no man than this, that a man
lay down his life for his friends."

JOHN 15:12–13

"Jesus said unto him, Thou shalt love the Lord
thy God with all thy heart, and with all thy soul,
and with all thy mind. This is the first and great
commandment. And the second is like unto
it, Thou shalt love thy neighbour as thyself."

MATTHEW 22:37–39

The Sign of God's Love

Jesus's presence on earth was an act of God's divine love. "For God so loved the world, that he gave his only begotten Son, that whosoever believeth in him should not perish, but have everlasting life" (John 3:16).

During Jesus's mortal ministry, He declared that the two greatest commandments are to love God and to love each other—even our enemies.

When He instituted the sacrament of the Lord's Supper, Jesus told His disciples that the true mark of their discipleship would be the love they displayed toward each other. Jesus's mortal life culminated in the supreme acts of love offered in Gethsemane and on the cross. During the Holy Week of Easter, we are reminded of the depth of Jesus's wondrous love and of His continued charge to "love one another; as I have loved you" (John 13:34).

THE KING OF LOVE MY SHEPHERD IS

Lyrics

The King of love my Shepherd is,
Whose goodness faileth never;
I nothing lack if I am His
And He is mine forever.

Where streams of living water flow,
My ransomed soul He leadeth;
And where the verdant pastures grow,
With food celestial feedeth.

Perverse and foolish, oft I strayed,
But yet in love He sought me;
And on His shoulder gently laid,
And home, rejoicing, brought me.

In death's dark vale I fear no ill,
With Thee, dear Lord, beside me;
Thy rod and staff my comfort still,
Thy cross before to guide me.

Thou spreadst a table in my sight;
Thy unction grace bestoweth;

And O what transport of delight
From Thy pure chalice floweth!

And so through all the length of days,
Thy goodness faileth never:
Good Shepherd, may I sing Thy praise
Within Thy house forever.

https://authormichaelyoung.com
/sacred-days-sacred-songs/

History

The words of Psalm 23 are enduring and familiar, and Henry Williams Baker drew upon them to write this hymn in the early nineteenth century.

Baker, an Anglican priest, wrote more than 300 hymns during his lifetime, including "Praise My Soul, the King of Heaven" and "The Church's One Foundation," but "The King of Love My Shepherd Is" is perhaps his most popular. The text was first published in 1868 in the hymnal *Hymns Ancient and Modern* and was set to the tune St. Columba, which is a traditional Irish melody. Over the years, however, it has been paired with a few different melodies. The lyrics themselves have been translated into many languages for churches around the world to sing.

In the hymn, Baker expresses his faith in God's care and provision for his life. He draws on the imagery of the shepherd and the sheep to convey the sense of security and peace he feels in God's presence. The hymn speaks of the streams of living water that God leads us beside, the verdant pastures where He feeds us, and the rod and staff that comfort us in times of trouble. As the King of love, Jesus promises that His love will follow us all the days of our lives (see Psalm 23:6).

O LOVE THAT WILL NOT LET ME GO

Lyrics

O Love that will not let me go,
I rest my weary soul in thee.
I give thee back the life I owe,
That in thine ocean depths its flow
May richer, fuller be.

O Light that follows all my way,
I yield my flick'ring torch to thee.
My heart restores its borrowed ray,
That in thy sunshine's blaze its day
May brighter, fairer be.

O Joy that seekest me through pain,
I cannot close my heart to thee.
I trace the rainbow through the rain,
And feel the promise is not vain,
That morn shall tearless be.

O Cross that liftest up my head,
I dare not ask to fly from thee.
I lay in dust, life's glory dead,
And from the ground there blossoms red,
Life that shall endless be.

https://authormichaelyoung.com
/sacred-days-sacred-songs/

History

This heartfelt hymn was born out of tragedy, yet it shows how Christ's love sustained the author through the most difficult period of his life.

"O Love, That Will Not Let Me Go" was written

by George Matheson in 1882. Matheson was born in Glasgow, Scotland, in 1842 and became a highly regarded theologian and preacher.

Matheson was engaged to be married when he lost his eyesight, and his fiancée broke off the engagement, which created additional agony for an already harrowing situation. The depth of his despair is clear in the last verse with the lyric, "I lay in dust, life's glory dead."

The hymn is said to have been written on the evening of Matheson's sister's wedding, a painful reminder of the love he himself had lost. The lyrics express a deep sense of trust and surrender to God's unfailing love and faithfulness, even amid difficult circumstances. The hymn evokes the imagery of beautiful things Matheson could no longer see, of "tracing the rainbow through the rain," "the sunshine's blaze," and the "blossom's red life."

Matheson lived a full and active life, and he is remembered for his contributions to theology, philosophy, and hymnody. This hymn reminds us that, regardless of the circumstances of our lives, the Savior's love will never let us go.

DAY SIX

GOOD FRIDAY

SACRIFICE

"And Isaac spake unto Abraham his father,
and said, . . . Behold the fire and the wood:
but where is the lamb for a burnt offering?
And Abraham said, My son, God will provide
himself a lamb for a burnt offering."

GENESIS 22:7–8

"Forasmuch as ye know that ye were not
redeemed with corruptible things, as silver
and gold, from your vain conversation
received by tradition from your fathers;
but with the precious blood of Christ, as
of a lamb without blemish and without
spot: who verily was foreordained before
the foundation of the world."

1 PETER 1:18–20

A Lamb without Blemish

The Old Testament recounts the story of Abraham, who was commanded by God to sacrifice his only son, Isaac, on an altar. Though Abraham was spared having to sacrifice his child, the event foreshadowed the time when God would provide a divine sacrificial lamb—His Only Begotten Son, Jesus Christ.

When the children of Israel were in bondage in Egypt, the Lord warned of a plague that would bring death to every firstborn son in the land. The Israelites were commanded to mark their doors with the blood of an unblemished, firstborn lamb in order for their sons to be spared (see Exodus 12). Just as the lamb's blood spared the Israelites from death, Christ's blood—as the Lamb of God—would eventually save all humanity from death.

When God established the Law of Moses among the Israelites, He commanded them to make burnt offerings to Him, including male lambs without blemish (see Leviticus 22:20). For more than thirteen hundred years, faithful Israelites offered unblemished lambs, looking forward to the time when God would provide Himself a lamb as foretold by the prophets.

Just as Isaac and many unblemished lambs were placed upon wood on an altar, Jesus was lifted on a wooden cross. The crown of thorns, the nails in His hands and feet, and the spear thrust into His side all shed His precious blood. In the sacrifice of His Son, God fulfilled Abraham's prophetic words by providing a Lamb that would save us all.

O SACRED HEAD NOW WOUNDED

Lyrics

O sacred Head now wounded,
With grief and shame weighed down,
Now scornfully surrounded
With thorns, thine only crown!

How art thou pale with anguish,
With sore abuse and scorn.
How does that visage languish,
Which once was bright as morn?

What language shall I borrow
To thank Thee, dearest friend?
For this, Thy dying sorrow,
Thy pity without end.

O make me thine forever,
And should I fainting be,
Lord, let me never, ever
Outlive my love to Thee.

https://authormichaelyoung.com
/sacred-days-sacred-songs/

History

Though this song has gone through many adaptations over the years, all the versions focus on the profound sacrifice that Christ made on the cross. This version comes to us through three different languages with similar thematic material.

The earliest iteration dates to the fourteenth century and comes from a longer Latin text, "Salve mundi salutare" ("Greetings, World, Greetings"), used in the Catholic church. Though it is not clear who the original author was, the hymn is sometimes attributed to the spiritual leader Bernard of Clairvaux.

The poem has seven different parts, each focusing on a unique part of the Savior's body, including His head, hands, feet, and side, and is structured to allow a different verse to be read or sung each day of the Holy Week.

When the Protestant Reformation began in Europe during the early 1500s, many Protestant denominations created their own versions of hymns by translating the text into the languages of their individual countries rather than singing everything in Latin.

In 1656, Paul Gerhardt translated the Latin text of this song into German. He adapted the final stanza to focus on Christ's head, describing the pain caused by the crown of thorns Jesus was forced to wear. His translation became known as "O Haupt voll Blut und Wunden," literally "O head full of blood and wounds," and was paired with a tune by the German composer Hans Leo Hassler. Hassler's tune, however, was originally meant to be sung as a secular song, "Mein Gemüth ist mir verwirret" ("My Mind Is in Confusion"), rather than a religious melody.

J. S. Bach later adapted Hassler's music, which is the tune we still sing today. Bach also adapted Hassler's tune with different harmonies in his musical work "St. Matthew's Passion," which used the Gospel of Matthew to tell the story of the Savior's death and Resurrection.

In 1830, Presbyterian minister James Waddell Alexander translated Gerhardt's German text into English under the name "O Sacred Head Now Wounded." This version gained widespread use in Protestant hymnbooks throughout the English-speaking world, and the song became especially popular during Good Friday services.

Today, there are many versions of this song, each sung in a variety of countries by a variety of singers, from soloists to small a cappella groups to large choirs. The song, with its haunting melody and poignant lyrics, has endured for hundreds of years perhaps because of the opportunity it provides Christians to ponder the magnitude of Christ's sacrifice, the reality of His own suffering, and His ability to comfort those who suffer.

WHEN I SURVEY THE WONDROUS CROSS

Lyrics

When I survey the wondrous cross
On which the Prince of Glory died,
My richest gain I count but loss
And pour contempt on all my pride.

Forbid it, Lord, that I should boast
Save in the death of Christ, my Lord.

All the vain things that charm me most,
I sacrifice them to His blood.

See from His head, His hands, His feet,
Sorrow and love flow mingled down.
Did ever such love and sorrow meet,
Or thorns compose so rich a crown?

Were the whole realm of nature mine,
That were an offering far too small.
Love so amazing, so divine,
Demands my soul, my life, my all!

An often omitted verse:

His dying crimson, like a robe,
Spreads o'er His body on the tree;
Then I am dead to all the globe,
And all the globe is dead to me.

https://authormichaelyoung.com
/sacred-days-sacred-songs/

History

This Easter favorite was written by Isaac Watts, one of the greatest hymn writers of all time. During his lifetime, he wrote more than 750 hymns, including "Joy to the World," "Sweet Is the Work," and "O God, Our Help in Ages Past." He was so influential that he is now referred to as "the Father of English hymnody."

Watts grew up the son of a minister in a dissenting congregation, which was a church that did not agree with the Church of England. He enjoyed the benefits of a rich education, which allowed him to become the pastor of his own congregation.

At the time, churches in England sang only texts directly based on Old Testament psalms, without any personal expressions of faith. Watts helped change that tradition by writing hymns that were both deeply personal and widely applicable. He wanted to sing hymns that matched the theme of the sermon, which meant he wrote many of them himself.

To make his new songs easier for his congregation to sing, he used the same meters—the number of syllables on each line—as the scriptural psalms so the unfamiliar words could be sung to familiar tunes.

"When I Survey the Wondrous Cross" first appeared in 1707 in the collection *Hymns and Spiritual Songs*. Over the years, it has been sung to a variety of tunes, but today, it is most often sung to a tune written by American hymn composer Lowell Mason and inspired by an old

Gregorian chant. Mason first paired the text of the hymn with his music in 1824.

This deeply introspective song allows us to imagine ourselves at the foot of the cross, pondering what Christ's loving sacrifice means for each of us. Each verse builds on the last, culminating in a powerful expression of devotion and faith.

Considering Christ's sacrifice for us helps us "pour contempt on all [our] pride" and encourages us to sacrifice "the vain things that charm [us] most." The love displayed by our Savior is so incredible that even if we could give Him "the whole realm of nature" it would be "a present far too small." This kind of divine love "demands my soul, my life, my all."

We cannot do enough to thank the Savior for what He sacrificed for us. But we can strive every day to make holy our souls, our lives, our all in His service.

DAY SEVEN

HOLY SATURDAY

OBEDIENCE

"For I came down from heaven, not to do mine
own will, but the will of him that sent me."

John 6:38

"And he went a little further, and fell on
his face, and prayed, saying, O my Father,
if it be possible, let this cup pass from me:
nevertheless not as I will, but as thou wilt."

Matthew 26:39

The Perfectly Obedient Son

Jesus Christ was the only perfectly obedient person who ever lived, even when that obedience led Him down difficult roads. Though He was without sin, He obeyed God's commandment to be baptized. When Satan tempted Jesus in the wilderness, Jesus remained obedient to God, even though He was hungry and tired from fasting for forty days. Then, when He knelt in Gethsemane, He offered the ultimate expression of obedience to God's will, saying "not my will, but thine, be done" (Luke 22:42). Although He had the power to save Himself from the agony He endured while on the cross, Jesus completed His holy mission.

This pattern of obedience provides a template for the rest of us. In every instance where Jesus obeyed His Father, blessings and miracles followed. As we choose to be obedient, we, too, can see the power of God blessing our lives.

WERE YOU THERE?

Lyrics

Were you there when they crucified my Lord?
Were you there when they crucified my Lord?
Oh, sometimes it causes me to tremble, tremble, tremble.
Were you there when they crucified my Lord?

Were you there when they nailed Him to the tree?
Were you there when they nailed Him to the tree?
Oh, sometimes it causes me to tremble, tremble, tremble.
Were you there when they nailed Him to the tree?

Were you there when they laid Him in the tomb?
Were you there when they laid Him in the tomb?
Oh, sometimes it causes me to tremble, tremble, tremble.
Were you there when they laid Him in the tomb?

Were you there when God raised Him from the tomb?
Were you there when God raised Him from the tomb?
Oh, sometimes it causes me to tremble, tremble, tremble.
Were you there when God raised Him from the tomb?

https://authormichaelyoung.com
/sacred-days-sacred-songs/

History

The exact origins of "Were You There When They Crucified My Lord?" is unknown, but it is believed to have been composed by enslaved African Americans in the United States during the early nineteenth century.

The hymn's lyrics describe the crucifixion of Jesus Christ and His obedience to His Father's will—giving Himself as a sacrifice for the salvation of humanity. The haunting melody and emotional lyrics not only speak to the intensity of Jesus's sacrifice but also intentionally included imagery that spoke to the brutality experienced by those who were enslaved. As the singer contemplates the depth of that divine sacrifice, it "causes [them] to tremble."

The song rose in popularity within Black communities throughout the nineteenth and early twentieth centuries. Its first publication was in 1899 in the book *Old Plantation Hymns*, a collection of popular spirituals compiled by William Eleazar Barton, an American writer, historian, and Congregationalist minister, as part of his effort to chronicle the history of slavery and the African American experience.

Throughout his career, Barton was a powerful advocate for abolition and civil rights. His most famous work is *The Soul of Abraham Lincoln*, which explores Lincoln's religious beliefs and their impact on his life and presidency. The book was a critical and commercial success and helped establish Barton as a leading authority of American history.

Over time, "Were You There When They Crucified My Lord?" became widely known and has been performed by musicians of all backgrounds, including Mahalia Jackson, Johnny Cash, and Joan Baez. It has also become a staple in many Christian denominations during Easter.

WORTHY IS THE LAMB

Lyrics

Worthy is the Lamb that was slain, and hath
redeemed us to God by His blood,
to receive power, and riches, and wisdom, and
strength, and honour, and glory, and blessing.
Blessing and honour, glory and power, be
unto Him that sitteth upon the throne, and
unto the Lamb, for ever and ever.
Amen.

https://authormichaelyoung.com
/sacred-days-sacred-songs/

History

The glorious celebration of the Savior's life, death, and Resurrection is at the heart of George Frederic Handel's masterpiece *Messiah*.

Charles Jennens, a wealthy Englishman and devout Christian, compiled the libretto and provided Handel with a text drawn entirely from Biblical passages in order to tell the entire story of the Messiah's mortal ministry and His Resurrection, as well as prophecies of His Second Coming.

Handel wrote much of the oratorio in a white-hot creative frenzy, working long hours at his desk and often neglecting meals and sleep. According to legend, when his servant brought him a meal after several days of intense work, Handel cried out, "I have it!" and rushed back to his writing. Another account states that when he reached the famous "Hallelujah Chorus," he exclaimed in the hearing of his assistant, "I think I did see heaven open, and the very face of God." He completed his work in just twenty-four days—from August 22 to September 14, 1741.

The work was first performed in Dublin in 1742 and was an immediate success. It has remained one of the most beloved and frequently performed choral works in the Western classical repertoire. Handel donated the proceeds of performances of *Messiah* to various charitable causes, from paying the debts of those in debtors' prison to a hospital that cared for orphans.

"Worthy Is the Lamb" is the finale of the oratorio, which celebrates Christ's triumph over death and His ascension to heaven. The words are from Revelation 5:12–14, which describes a vision of a scroll with seven seals that only the Lamb of God, who was slain and resurrected, can open.

Jesus showed His worthiness by doing His Father's will, and He invites all of us to follow His glorious example.

DAY EIGHT

EASTER SUNDAY

RENEWAL

"Now upon the first day of the week, very early in the morning, they came unto the sepulchre, bringing the spices which they had prepared, and certain others with them. And they found the stone rolled away from the sepulchre. And they entered in, and found not the body of the Lord Jesus. And it came to pass, as they were much perplexed thereabout, behold, two men stood by them in shining garments: And as they were afraid, and bowed down their faces to the earth, they said unto them, Why seek ye the living among the dead? He is not here, but is risen."

LUKE 24:1–6

"[Mary] turned herself back, and saw Jesus standing, and knew not that it was Jesus. Jesus saith unto her, Woman, why weepest thou? whom seekest thou? She, supposing him to be the gardener, saith unto him, Sir, if thou have borne him hence, tell me where thou hast laid him, and I will take him away. Jesus saith unto her, Mary. She turned herself, and saith unto him, Rabboni; which is to say, Master."

JOHN 20:14–16

Beauty for Ashes

During Jesus's ministry, He referenced Isaiah 61:3, "To appoint unto them that mourn in Zion, to give unto them beauty for ashes, the oil of joy for mourning, the garment of praise for the spirit of heaviness; that they might be called trees of righteousness, the planting of the Lord, that he might be glorified."

When something is in ashes, it has been completely destroyed, and it takes miraculous power to change those ashes into something beautiful. But that is exactly what our Savior promises us—complete renewal, even after our lives end and our bodies have turned to dust.

For Mary Magdalene, she experienced a different kind of renewal. Upon meeting the resurrected Lord in the garden on that first Easter Sunday, her deep despair was replaced with unspeakable joy the moment she recognized Him.

We do not have to wait until after this life or for a miraculous manifestation to be renewed by the Savior's power. When we ask for and receive forgiveness, when we find hope in times of despair, or when we are able to be healed from deep spiritual wounds, we can be renewed. The promise of Easter morning is that no loss need be permanent and that all sorrow is temporary. This is the

glorious gift offered to all who will turn their hearts to
Jesus Christ.

IN THE GARDEN

Lyrics

I come to the garden alone
While the dew is still on the roses,
And the voice I hear, falling on my ear,
The Son of God discloses.

And He walks with me,
And He talks with me,
And He tells me I am His own,
And the joy we share as we tarry there
None other has ever known.

He speaks and the sound of His voice
Is so sweet the birds hush their singing,
And the melody that He gave to me
Within my heart is ringing.

And He walks with me,
And He talks with me,
And He tells me I am His own,

And the joy we share as we tarry there
None other has ever known.

I'll stay in the garden with Him
Though the night around me is falling.
But He bids me go, through the voice of woe
His voice to me is calling.

And He walks with me,
And He talks with me,
And He tells me I am His own,
And the joy we share as we tarry there
None other has ever known.
None other has ever known.

https://authormichaelyoung.com
/sacred-days-sacred-songs/

History

Author C. Austin Miles was once described in these words: "He looked a little like a southern colonel with his white mustache and a small flower in his lapel. His extraordinary sense of humor and dry wit could be very caustic if he thought the occasion demanded it—a truly brilliant man."

Now this might sound more like someone who

should be selling fried chicken than writing religious songs, but "In the Garden" has been an enduring favorite among Christian congregations ever since it was written in 1912. It first gained widespread popularity during the Billy Sunday evangelical campaigns, and it has been recorded by a variety of artists, including Tennessee Ernie Ford, Doris Day, the Statler Brothers, Mahalia Jackson, and Brad Paisley. More than a million copies of it have been sold around the world.

Miles did not start off as a musician, however, having initially attended the Philadelphia College of Pharmacy and the University of Pennsylvania. After deciding that career was not for him, he published a gospel song with the Hall-Mack Company. He eventually worked for them as an editor and manager for the next thirty-seven years.

He said, "It is as a writer of gospel songs I am proud to be known, for in that way I may be of the most use to my master, whom I serve willingly although not as efficiently as is my desire."

He was also an avid photographer and built a darkroom in his basement where he would often read the Bible under the red lights while he waited for photos to develop. Inspiration came one night while he was reading in John 20 about Mary Magdalene, who came to the Garden Tomb only to find Jesus missing and then to learn of His Resurrection. She is moved from heartbreak to joy. Likewise, "In the Garden" allows the singer and the listener to contemplate meeting the resurrected Savior and being able to spend some time one-on-one with Him. It is a deeply personal application of scripture. Miles wrote both the lyrics and the music that same night.

Miles said of the song, "This is not an experience limited to a happening almost 2,000 years ago. It is the daily companionship with the Lord that makes up the Christian's life."

CHRIST THE LORD IS RISEN TODAY

Lyrics

Christ the Lord is ris'n today, Alleluia!
Sons of men and angels say, Alleluia!
Raise your joys and triumphs high, Alleluia!
Sing, ye heav'ns, and earth reply, Alleluia!

Love's redeeming work is done, Alleluia!
Fought the fight, the vict'ry won, Alleluia!

Jesus' agony is o'er, Alleluia!
Darkness veils the earth no more, Alleluia!

Lives again our glorious King, Alleluia!
Where, O death, is now thy sting? Alleluia!
Once He died our souls to save, Alleluia!
Where thy victory, O grave? Alleluia!

https://authormichaelyoung.com
/sacred-days-sacred-songs/

History

This classic Easter hymn can be traced back through Charles Wesley, the cofounder of the Methodist church, who based his work—"Hymn for Easter Day"—on an earlier Bohemian hymn, "Jesus Christ Is Risen Today," which itself can be linked to a fourteenth-century Latin hymn.

"Christ the Lord Is Risen Today" was first heard at the inaugural service for the first Methodist chapel, the Foundery Meeting House, before being published in the hymnal *Hymns and Sacred Poems*. The song broke from the traditional hymns of the day, which were often paraphrases of scripture with a more solemn tone and music, by evoking a joyful, uplifting feeling. In addition, the text is written in present tense, which gives a sense of including not only those who lived in Christ's day but also those who live today.

In Wesley's original version, the song had eleven verses with four lines apiece, but it is now usually reduced to four to six verses, depending on the hymnal. There was a tradition among the Roman Catholic and Anglican churches to refrain from using the word "Alleluia" in their services during Lent and then begin using it again on Easter Sunday, which might explain why the "Alleluia" refrain began to appear in hymnals during the early nineteenth century.

Like many hymns, the text has been set to a variety of tunes over the years. The most popular is called EASTER HYMN, which is an anonymous tune that appeared in *Lyrica Davidica* in 1708. It has also been sung to the tunes LLANFAIR, SAVANNAH, and RESURREXIT.

"Be of good cheer;
I have overcome the world."

—JOHN 16:33

Sources

INTRODUCTION

Victor Hugo Quotes. *BrainyQuote.com* (website). Available at https://www.brainyquote.com/quotes/victor_hugo _106867; accessed May 3, 2023.

DAY 1

Hatchett, Marion J. *Commentary on the American Prayer Book.* HarperCollins, 1995.

"The Holy City" (blog post), 12 December 2020. *Croydon Hills & Wonga Park Anglican Church* (website). Available at https://www.chawpac.org.au/post/the-holy-city; accessed 3 May 2023.

"The Holy City." *Hymnary.org* (website). Available at https:// hymnary.org/text/last_night_i_lay_a_sleeping; accessed 3 May 2023.

"John Mason Neale." *The Canterbury Dictionary of Hymnology* (website). Available at https://hymnology.hymnsam .co.uk/j/john-mason-neale?q=john%20mason%20neale; accessed 3 May 2023.

Julian, John. *A Dictionary of Hymnology.* Dover Publications, 1957.

Weatherly, Frederic. *Songs of Frederic Weatherly.* Hodder and Stoughton, 1929.

Young, Carlton R. *Companion to the United Methodist Hymnal.* Abingdon Press, 1993.

DAY 2

"Drop, Drop Slow Tears." *Hymnary.org* (website). Available at https://hymnary.org/text/drop_drop_slow_tears; accessed 3 May 2023.

Gounod, Charles. "O Divine Redeemer! (Repentir)." London: Novello & Co., 1904.

Julian, John, ed. *A Dictionary of Hymnology: Setting Forth the Origin and History of Christian Hymns of All Ages and Nations.* New York: Charles Scribner's Sons, 1892. Reprint: Legare Street Press, 2022.

Newell, Lloyd. "Scene in the Form of a Prayer." *Music and the Spoken Word.* Available at https://www.deseret.com/2017/9 /30/20620545/music-and-the-spoken-word-scene-in-the -form-of-a-prayer; accessed 3 May 2023.

Osbeck, Kenneth W. *Amazing Grace: 366 Inspiring Hymn Stories for Daily Devotions.* Grand Rapids, MI: Kregel Publications, 1990.

"Phineas Fletcher." *Encyclopedia Britannica* (website). Available at https://www.britannica.com/biography/Phineas-Fletcher; accessed 3 May 2023.

DAY 3

"Come, Thou Fount of Every Blessing." *Hymnary.org* (website). Available at https://hymnary.org/text/come_thou_fount _of_every_blessing; accessed 3 May 2023.

Hawn, C. Michael. "History of Hymns: 'Come, thou Fount of every blessing." *Discipleship Ministries: The United Methodist Church* (website). Available at https://www.umc discipleship.org/resources/history-of-hymns-come-thou -fount-of-every-blessing; accessed 3 May 2023.

Newton, John. *Thoughts upon the African Slave Trade.* London, J. Buckland, 1788.

"Robert Robinson." *Wikipedia.org* (website). Available at https://en.wikipedia.org/wiki/Robert_Robinson_(Baptist); ac-cessed 11 February 2022.

Terry, Lindsay. "Story behind the song: 'Come Thou Fount.'" *The St. Augustine Record* (website). Available at https://www .staugustine.com/story/lifestyle/faith/2015/09/17/story -behind-song-come-thou-fount/16263811007/; accessed 3 May 2023.

DAY 4

"Edward Mote." *Hymnology Archive* (website). Available at https://www.hymnologyarchive.com/edward-mote; ac-cessed 3 May 2023.

Mote, Edward. "The Immutable Basis of a Sinner's Hope." *Hymns of Praise: A New Selection of Gospel Hymns.* London: Edward Mote, 1836.

"My Hope Is Built on Nothing Less." *Hymnary.org* (website). Available at https://hymnary.org/text/my_hope_is_built _on_nothing_less; accessed 3 May 2023.

"The Solid Rock" (lyrics). *Timeless Truths.org* (website). Available at https://library.timelesstruths.org/music/The _Solid_Rock/; accessed 3 May 2023.

Terry, Lindsay. "Story behind the song: It is well with my soul."

The St. Augustine Record (website). Available at https://www.staugustine.com/story/lifestyle/faith/2014/10/17/story-behind-song-it-well-my-soul/985525007/; accessed 3 May 2023.

"The Touching Story behind 'It Is Well with My Soul.'" *The Tabernacle Choir Blog.* Available at https://www.thetabernaclechoir.org/articles/it-is-well-with-my-soul.html; accessed 3 May 2023.

DAY 5

Hawn, C. Michael. "History of Hymns: 'O Love That Wilt Not Let Me Go.'" *Discipleship Ministries: The United Methodist Church* (website). Available at https://www.umcdiscipleship.org/resources/history-of-hymns-o-love-that-wilt-not-let-me-go; accessed 3 May 2023.

Jarrett, Katie. "History of Hymns: 'The King of Love My Shepherd Is.'" *Discipleship Ministries: The United Methodist Church* (website). Available at https://www.umcdiscipleship.org/resources/history-of-hymns-the-king-of-love-my-shepherd-is; accessed 3 May 2023.

Matheson, George. "O Love That Wilt Not Let Me Go." *The Cyber Hymnal* (website). Available at http://www.hymntime.com/tch/htm/o/l/t/w/oltwnlmg.htm; accessed 3 May 2023.

Ortlund, Dane. "O Love That Will Not Let Me Go." *The Gospel Coalition* (website). Available at https://www.thegospelcoalition.org/blogs/justin-taylor/o-love-that-will-not-let-me-go/; accessed 3 May 2023.

Osbeck, Kenneth W. *Amazing Grace: 366 Inspiring Hymn Stories for Daily Devotions.* Kregel Publications, 1990.

"What are the lyrics to 'The king of love my shepherd is'?" *Classical Music* (website) Available at https://www.classical-music.com/features/articles/the-king-of-love-my-shepherd-is-lyrics/; accessed 3 May 2023.

DAY 6

Richter, Kyle. "What Happened on Good Friday? A Timeline of Jesus's Last Day." *The Crossing* (website). Available at https://info.thecrossingchurch.com/blog/what-happened-on-good-friday-a-timeline-of-jesuss-crucifixion; accessed 3 May 2023.

Sowa, Joseph. "The Musical History of 'O Savior, Thou Who Wearest.'" *Joseph Sowa: Composer, Scholar, Coach* (website). Available at https://josephsowa.com/musical-history-o-savior-thou-who-wearest/; accessed 3 May 2023.

Tillay, Rachel. "History of Hymns: 'When I Survey the Wondrous Cross.'" *Discipleship Ministries: The United Methodist Church* (website). Available at https://www.umcdiscipleship.org/resources/history-of-hymns-when-i-survey-the-wondrous-cross; accessed 3 May 2023.

Waters, Michael W. "History of Hymns: 'O sacred Head, now wounded.'" *Discipleship Ministries: The United Methodist Church* (website). Available at https://www.umcdiscipleship.org/resources/history-of-hymns-o-sacred-head-now-wounded-1; accessed 3 May 2023.

"When I Survey the Wondrous Cross." *The Tabernacle Choir Blog.* Available at https://www.thetabernaclechoir.org/articles/when-i-survey-the-wondrous-cross.html; accessed 3 May 2023.

DAY 7

Barton, William E. *The Soul of Abraham Lincoln.* New York: George H. Doran, 1920.

Bjorlin, David. "History of Hymns: 'Were You There.'" *Discipleship Ministries: The United Methodist Church* (website). Available at https://www.umcdiscipleship.org/resources /history-of-hymns-were-you-there; accessed 3 May 2023.

Burrows, Donald. *Handel.* 2nd Edition. Oxford University Press, 2010.

Dean, Winton. *Handel's Messiah: The Texts and Their Sources.* Washington, DC: Amadeus Press, 1993.

Handel, George Frideric. *Messiah.* Edited by Watkins Shaw. London: Novello, 1959.

Walker, Wayne S. "Were You There?" *Hymn Studies Blog* (website). Available at https://hymnstudiesblog.wordpress .com/2015/08/06/were-you-there/; accessed 3 May 2023.

DAY 8

Fenner, Chris. "In the Garden." *Hymnology Archive* (website). Available at https://www.hymnologyarchive.com/in-the -garden; accessed 3 May 2023.

Hawn, C. Michael. "History of Hymns: 'Christ the Lord Is Risen Today.'" *Discipleship Ministries: The United Methodist Church* (website). Available at https://www.umcdiscipleship .org/articles/history-of-hymns-christ-the-lord-is-risen -today; accessed 3 May 2023.

Rushford, Jerry. "Hymns of the Season: Christ the Lord Is Risen Today." *Pepperdine Library News* (website). Available at https://library.pepperdine.edu/news/posts/hymns

-of-the-season-christ-the-lord-is-risen-today.htm; accessed 3 May 2023.

Terry, Lindsay. "Story behind the song: 'In the Garden.'" *The St. Augustine Record* (website). Available at https://www .staugustine.com/story/lifestyle/faith/2015/03/05/story -behind-song-garden/16247416007/; accessed 3 May 2023.

About the Author

Though Michael grew up traveling the world with his military father, he now lives in Utah with his wife, Jen, and their three children. He played for several years with the handbell choir Bells on Temple Square and is now a member of The Tabernacle Choir at Temple Square. He is the author of the novels in The Canticle Kingdom series, The Last Archangel series, the Chess Quest series, and the Penultimate Dawn Cycle (The Hunger), as well as several non-fiction works, including *An Advent Carols Countdown*, *The Song of the Righteous*, and *As Saints We Sing*. Learn more at www.authormichaelyoung.com.